Moments of
Light

M C Thorne

Foreword

These poems have been written over a period of more than forty years. Having assembled and reviewed them, I have altered very little. Although the subject matter has changed somewhat with time, I find the poems written when I was twenty neither superior nor inferior to those written recently. For this collection, I have arranged the material in alphabetical order, since chronology of composition did not seem relevant and no arrangement by topic entirely satisfied me.

Some of the poems express my personal feelings. However, the reader should be aware that a poet, like a novelist, is an inventor of scenes and that the speaker in a poem may, or may not, be the author. Nevertheless, whether emerging from natural feeling or contrived by artifice, throughout the aim is to express something that touches upon truth, even if one has to sneak up upon it obliquely.

Most of the poems in this collection are straightforward and require little commentary. However, there are a few where some knowledge of the background may be helpful. For this reason, I have provided short footnotes, as appropriate. However, even in these cases, I think that the poems stand by themselves and that the meaning for an individual reader should emerge from his or her engagement with the text.

I have said that some of these poems express my personal feelings. In particular, a few were written expressly for my beloved wife, who has been my companion, friend and helper throughout the period of their composition. To her I dedicate this volume – without her, I would be less of a person and this would be less of a book.

Mike Thorne

Hamsterley, County Durham, UK

19 June 2013

Contents

A Big Issue

A quid would have been good,
I could've got a drink for a quid;
Sat in the pub for hours,
Washed in the loo with their soap
And warmed myself through.
Yeah – a quid would have been good.

How did I get on the streets?
Well, home was a mess,
There's not much work when you're thick
And the leg that I broke as a kid
Never mended the way it should
And I wanted to see some life.

Did I get a quid? What do you think?
Two guys in suits, with their ties
All neatly tied – what do you think?
Nah! Not a penny, but still
After the big one jerked me on my feet
My knee didn't hurt, I didn't need a drink.

His name? Peter, I think. His friend was John.
You know them? Well give them my best;
I'm off up north to me mam's to start again.

A Birth

The gentle winds of early Spring
Deepen the silence of the night.
The muted softness of the light
Makes distant cares that dawn may bring.
A solemn and a holy thing
Is come to pass, they sleep at last,
Safe from the storm, in harbour fast,
While I their hymn of praise may sing,
An aubade to this early birth.
She who was one is now made twain
And each is loved as was the one.
To both the joys of fruitful Earth
And also all her cares again.
God bless them both, under the sun.

A Glass of Wine

The colour is its beauty
And the hands
That cluster ghostlike
All about my glass.

Such pressings of the grape
Our fathers had
And Socrates
Before he drank and died.

The colour is its beauty
And the hands
That cluster ghostlike
All about my glass.

Death comes to all
And others pour the wine
Into the transient glass
And drink and die.

An Advertisement for Gawain and the Green Knight

Ages ago, when Arthur Albion ruled,
In seasonal celebration, when he sat
At table, would not test or try or taste
A morsel of his meal until some marvel made
In his rich realm was recounted or rehearsed.

Thus, when New Year his natal day announced
And all on dais with due dignity disposed,
Where bright bedecked blazons in banners hung,
So Arthur sat and would not suffer service.

Then, suddenly surprising, sore strokes upon the door
Presaged the presence of a perilous person,
All girt in green, of stature great and gruesome,
From throat to thigh, thickset and terrible,
His loins immense, and limbs both long and large.

Tedious it were to tell one tithe of the trifles
That bedecked his body in bounteous abandon.
On his steed in his stirrups he stood, astride the threshold,
Threatening and terrible he turned to the high table.

Then Arthur, all amazed, authority displayed
And courteously commanded that the curious creature
Briefly his business bring before the court.

'May he that sits in highest heaven help me',
Began the knight in green with gentle grace,
'Be bold in bringing you both burden and bargain.
Constrained at Christmas to contrive a contest,
Bold barons all, I'll bear such a blow
As any here with axe will dare address,
So long as I, in Lent, when new leaves lengthen,
Can so respond by smiting him the same.'

All sat amazed, no answer was assayed,
'Til gallant Gawain, goaded, Arthur's guest,
Stood and spoke thus 'Sir will I so strike
And knick thy neck, that never another stroke
Will you deliver, I do defy you – let the deal be done.'

So the green giant knelt and Gawain grasped
The axe, ash-shafted, angled it aloft
And with a shuddering stroke the sinews slashed
Such that the helmeted head in haste was hewn
From the broad body, and bounced upon the bench.

Yet marvel upon marvel, the man moved.
He rose, he reached, his riven head removed
From the flagged floor; then one foot he placed
In his steed's stirrup, into the saddle sprang
And spoke to Gawain, as he gasped and goggled,
'Now I depart, do you not dare delay,
At Lent I now command you come and cleave
To corresponding chance at the green chapel.'

My essay now ends here, but each event
That followed, how Gawain's fortune fared,
Are told in total by a trusty talent,
Elsewhere. His record you should read.

At the Gate

What song shall I sing you,
You whom dance is moving?
Shall I sing of sunrise,
Or grass in the morning?
Shall I sing of sunset,
When the leaves have fallen?
Shall I make you music
On the pipe or tabor?
What song shall I sing you,
You whom dance is moving?
Shall I sing of cut glass,
Coloured light refracting,
Or the leaf light moving
In the woodland noontide?
What song shall I sing you,
Moving in your dancing?
See, I have no music
And my pipe is broken.

Autumnal

This the beginning of long winter hours,
Substantial by our Sunday, tea-time fires,
But, outside, smoke from dying garden pyres
Curls in the air.
Replete with scones and cake, we should not stare
To where
A pageant passes in the cobweb dusk.
(God-given spirit fled, only the baser husk
In darkness darkly flowers.)

Dust in their mouths they mime their piteous cries,
Jocasta for twice-nurtured Oedipus sighs,
But Thebes is only grass and weathered stone
And, under the stone, the dead with shuttered eyes.

Now the beginning of long winter hours,
The flames form petals of impossible flowers
And flicker out.
The shadows on the wall
Falter and fall
Into a tangible darkness like a cloak.

Where is the substance that I have consumed,
The delicacies, the books on weighty matters?
Why is our conversation not resumed
And why does no-one make their tea cup clatter?

The soul that I once had is surely flown
And I am left, bereft, on Earth alone,
In that eternal procession to take my place
And cover up my non-existent face.

Bern, 1986

You would not think that you were near the mountains,
Where ornate clocks tell out the urban hours
Amongst stout buildings, window-boxed with flowers,
With water channelled feeding civic fountains.

Yet, high across the Aare you see them ragged
Along the skyline, in wet mist enfolded;
Nearer at hand the wooded slopes are moulded
To human scale; but the high Alps stand jagged.

We would be sober, safe in patterned hours,
Amongst the ordered ranks of serried flowers,
Content with limited freedom, constrained passion,
While abdicating choice to current fashion;
But the peaks stand – and standing break the pattern.

Beyond the Air

Beyond the air perennial silence lies
And the noise of man, in silence, silent dies.
The BBC fades into solar hiss
And all our vain creation comes to this,
A dying whimper in a vast abyss.

Beyond the air the creatures of our night
Burn in their cosmic dance with glowing light.
Yet, white stars turn to red and soon grow cold,
The universe itself is growing old,
Voraciously the dark the light enfolds.

Beyond the air perennial silence lies,
But we are here, a single curlew cries,
The light of morning seeps through shuttered eyes;
And, speaking in the waves upon the shore,
He murmers 'I am with you evermore'.

'Though matter fail and hope turn to despair,
Though you are blind and deaf, still I am here,
So, trust in me, and put away all fear.'
Then I, with lightened heart, get out of bed,
Put on the kettle and make toast of bread.

Black Loch

When the late evening light unmoving stood
Before the sudden plunge of northern night,
Upon each eminence and lofty height
A late breeze moved the wood.
Far off, the sea its murmerous motion rolled
Upon the outcrops of a northern shore,
Telling the tale of all its treasured store
Of natural wonders and of patterned gold.
Between two headlands the receding tide
Troubled the turbid waters between towers
Of weathered rock.
The gnarled trees, in deep fissures on each side,
Whispered a litany, dropping their frail flowers
On the black loch.

Bridges

I was a builder and my bridges grew
In arching spans from isle to either bank,
So traffic multiplied and trade grew rich
In commerce of men's fertile minds and loves.

Then said I 'let these other men repair
And paint and mend these bridges I have built,
For I will rest a while and take my ease
In this safe haven at the heart of all.'

But men went elsewhere, and by slow decay
Bridges became unsafe, their traffic waned
And streets once noisy with commingled thought
Echoed the lone pedestrian as he walked
Between the empty warehouses that once
Contained such stores as wise men's hearts delight.

Slow is the social failure, we connect
Less with each other and the highways run
By other bridges, ours are broken down
Leaving us lone, the guardians of an isle
Where ruinous decay mocks our best dreams
And only ghosts of all our high ideals
Lurk in the corners, where the dust lies deep.

By Rail over Penistone

Beneath a skin of earth the rock is there,
Its sharp-faced edges rise and fall away,
And after passions fail the rocks are here,
The rocks beneath the skin remain and stay.

Here are the scanty pastures, highland sheep,
And last remains of snow on the sharp peaks.
Still by the broken sheep cote it lies deep
And through its roof the sullen rainfall leaks.

No human habitation in this gale
That screams down broken gullies in the hills.
With outpost far below, in grey-faced cotton mills,
Humanity falters, stumbles, falls and fails.
Beneath a skin of earth the rock is there,
Beyond our span the rocks remain and stay.

Cawdor Castle

Over the moonlit waters
The owl with piercing cry
From near to further woodland
Is black against the sky.

The dark-walled castle towers
Over the rocky burn,
While bats with secret voices
Wheel and dip and turn.

The light behind a window
Flickers and fades to dark;
As dark as the castle courtyard
And near-deserted park.

The sound of the tumbling waters,
The scent of the evening flowers,
Come to the one who listens
To the tower clock tell the hours.

The dead of night is coming,
The air is black and thick,
Piled high the weeds are rotting,
Their breath comes sweet and sick.

The postern door is open,
Although the hour is late;
The shape that slips unnoticed
Moves with the motion of fate.

The dark behind a window
Flickers and grows to light,
Before it fades to blackness
In the deep dark dead of night.

Over the moonlit waters
The hunter returns with his prey;
The actions that night has encompassed
Await the break of day.

Say not that the evil perish,
The truth is far more stark,
He who wills, his will can accomplish,
Who moves with his fate in the dark.

Chanctonbury Ring

When last I stood upon this high hill's top
You could see miles, a little blue maybe
In the far distance, but the fields all fell
Beneath my feet and the low winter sun
Shone warm on grass that sheep had lately cropped.
That was last week, but now I am enclosed
By sheets of rain, the wind whips in my face;
Sensible sheep and trippers are indoors,
But I have climbed the steep and muddy track
To feel the icy wind and fail to see,
Though I can hear it near, the suffering wood.
Why have I climbed and slipped and cursed the mud,
Got frozen fingers and a running nose;
To feel as those original dwellers felt
Who braved all weathers here, and bears and wolves,
Or to be one with nature? Neither thought
Was in my heart, rather in this bleak place
To turn into myself and feel the pulse
Of my uniqueness in a wintry world.
Strange that I should write
These few short lines, half believing that I stood
A second time by Chanctonbury Ring.
In truth, I stood there once and all the rest
Are fireside dreams made on a wintry night.
But not for nothing have I conjured here,
For dreams are nearer now than is the real
Remembered visit and the thoughts it woke;
And no-one has to wash my muddy clothes.

Note: Chanctonbury Ring is an iron-age hill-fort on the South Downs.

Chichester Harbour

I have seen the masts, like lances from afar,
Rising over the skyline, swaying to and fro,
Gulls have hovered above them, soundless in the sky,
Can you tell me where, or why it is, they go?

I have seen the trees sway in autumn skies,
Whipped by a wintry breeze from off the northern shore.
I have seen the laughter die out of your eyes,
Can you tell me where, or why, the light has gone?

Cotter and Son

There were no matters that he had not thought
Were sorted out and ordered, bottles set
In serried ranks and labelled to his will,
Powders in folded paper, the pressed pills
In cardboard pots, and eye drops with pipettes.

A syrup for a cough,
A salve for wounds,
An ointment for an eczema perhaps,
Or ammoniac salts to stimulate,
Or..., but what can stay
The enormous flood of grief,
Or can unsay
The trestled coffin in an upstairs room,
Long surge of mourners down a village street.

The shutters must be lowered,
All too soon
He will go out with stepladder and brush
And change the sign
To 'Cotter' only; so delete the son.

Drought in August

All day the river has been busy with traffic,
The motor boats, the fat in family parties,
Young men and girls in yachts, children's canoes;
But now it is evening,
The kingfisher flashes green in the pool
And the silent vortices move in the slow-moving waters,
While the waterweed bubbles its breath
To the evening air.
Proceeding and unchanging here,
The river runs around its easy bend.

Still pools beneath the willow trees,
Where clouds of midges slip the breeze
And promenade in evening air
Above the heavy pike's cool lair.

The fields are deep with summer grass,
Where venturing gulls pass and repass.
A fish turns over on its side,
The rushes gently bend and sway,
And all the waters of the day
Are gone away,
Lost in the deep of lunar tide,
Are moving out across the wide
North Sea, to Dogger, where the herring ride
In their massed ranks.

The waters move without a sound
Toward the sea in which they're drowned.

———————————

Artesian wells are running dry,
All hopes of rain the skies belie,
Cut flowers wilt in cut-glass vase
And people may not wash their cars.

———————————

Now in the fields the stubble chars and reeks,
The black smoke billows up against the sky,
The ground is dry.

Green becomes withered yellow in the drought,
The flint of church walls burning to the hand,
A dusty land.

Here, steady paced, the country women stoop,
Picking the bushes over once again;
August, and no rain.

The heavy afternoon moves on with gasping breath,
In a great room of hanging, grey-blue cloud
With insects loud.

———————————

The summer bleached by heat and purged of motion,
Absence of thought and absence of emotion;
The river waters flow,
The pickers move from row to weary row.

Easter Saturday

Here a space of quiet hours,
Clear skies above the rain-blessed branch,
A time of scented evening flowers.

Here a stillness before growing
Awareness in the warm dark earth,
The wakening of autumn sowing.

This is the garden and the tomb,
White rock among the weeping trees
Defines his temporary home.

What need of ointment or of balm,
He sleeps in silence, without breath,
In the peaceful twilight calm.

Here a space of quiet hours,
A life is ended, not begun,
Among the scented evening flowers.

And in this space between the times of motion,
Time passes, as in a peaceful ocean
Each similar wave performs a slight erosion.

Now, without noticed change, the empty tomb,
Time is renewed and life begun anew.
The early sunlight pierces the mist through.
We see the open door and vacant room
Revealed, as is each opening bloom.
Thus is his promise to us all made true.
By death his marvellous stature changed and grew,
And he himself becomes the open door
That leads to life with him for evermore.
He becomes all, the way, the truth, the life,
The fount of peace after all toil and strife,
The boundless love that will prepare our place
Within his father's house of perfect grace.

Evening Praise

Lord, at my shoulder all this day
You stood to keep my fears at bay,
Now, in the evening, by my side,
Strength in my weakness, you abide.
No step I make but in you Lord,
By angels and by me adored,
Who, by your Father's impulse moved,
Made this creation that I love.
And when by sin I was estranged
You brought me home, my life you changed
From worthlessness to your delight,
Brought out of darkness into light.

Fenland Sunday

Windmills and churches from the landscape rise,
Matt black against the iridescent skies.
The Sunday evening bells bound and rebound
Across the miles of undeviating ground.
Cries
Of the birds that flap across the marsh
Are harsh
And shrill,
As evening hunters seek un-needed kill.

Here is a single plant of the wild rose
And heather warm with the remembered sun,
Along the path a quiet party goes,
Their joy in God with nature here begun.

Christ crucified burns in my head like fire.
The honest merchant a domestic liar,
The gentle man who leaves his lover flat,
The child whose play is torturing the cat.
We murder God by trivial desire
And yet our sins within our God expire.

The guns are silent, mist is in the air,
Across the marsh a plaintive last bird call
Numbers the dead, the hunters disappear,
In an immensity man is very small.

Five Finger Exercise

His girl is here; he is glad she is sure,
Her dress is red and she has fair hair.
Her lad fills a jug from a cold dark rill,
High over the hill shrills a lark in the air.

Now fall the leaves; he had a rug,
Her dress was red, he was glad she was sure;
The jug that he filled is broken and lost,
But the hills endure.

Flood

Here the soft darkness where the willows weep
In slumber deep.
The iridescent waters gently flow
And cast a silver glow.

A distant church bell tells a single chime
In marking time.
There is the murmur of a stirring breeze
Ruffling the trees.

The gathering clouds, briefly, obscure the moon,
Far off the groan
Of the deep-moving sea across the mere
And sandhills bare.

A single spot of rain ripples the stream,
Breaks its smooth gleam
And the mad branches dip in opening dance
With frantic glance.

The wind whistles and whines across the ground.
With deeper sound
The sea gathers its rippling muscles and breaks
Against protective stakes.

The rain comes sleeting hard, in rods of steel,
There is only the feel
Of the rain and the foam and the pounding surf on the beach,
Only the feel of each.

Here is the crumbling sand and rotting wood
That many a sea withstood,
Until the ocean showed its full ferocious power
In this primeval hour.

Sands flow and run like water in this gale,
Defences break and fail;
Farmlands and cattle deep in rolling waves
Among the sailors' graves.

Here is soft darkness where the willows weep
In slumber deep.
The once sweet earth is salt to taste
And the sweet pasture waste.

Genesis

Hasten and hear all who would hearken and heed
To the tale of time, as told by a teller of truth
Who has watched the war lords wend down weary years,
Magnificent men all marred and marked for death.
Hearken and hear of woe and a world's winning,
The sweetness and strength of sorrow for salvation.
Listen, to learn and live, you noble Lordings,
To best beginnings broken and better bargains.

Before all things began, unbroken blackness,
Absolute absence of all, antedated creation;
Position and place were absent, past and present were not,
And nothing was known in that negation of nature.
Only, over it all, in outermost darkness,
A presence of power purposed, perceived and planned,
Conceived and created a concept; this creation,
Transforming in time, with energy turbulent tossed,
Seething with stars spread in superabundance,
Became and was born, because the act of begetting
Made manifest the might of the great mover,
Maker of worlds, and men, and men's good doing.

Poured in all parts the power of that prime mover;
Planets were placed by laws in predestined positions,
Spinning in space around some stabler stars,
Barren and bare and burning among the beacons,
The blazing brands that brought before and after.
Surfaces sere and stark solidified slowly,
Cracked and contorted, convulsed sometimes with craters,
Cooled and congealed to a distinct definition.
On Earth, events were such as elsewhere ended
In gaunt dead globes, grey and grimed with dust;
But here the maker's hand with a high hauteur
Forthwith caused fowl and fish to flourish forth,
Planted and planned, prepared a Paradise
Well stocked with all the good that a world wanted.

27

Beasts in abundance, birds he also brought forth,
Grass of the greenest, growing garlands of flowers,
Fine new forests and fields, by water flowing
In shifting sparkles under the summer sun.
Beeches and birches, above the brakes and brambles,
Potential pasture and ploughland, in wild perfection,
By Autumn, brimful of berries in blissful abundance.

This world, fully furnished, lacked that which was finally fitting,
The namer of names, newest of this new creation,
Man the maker, mover of his own motions,
Forced to consider a choice of contingent conditions,
Dubious debater, ever disturbed by doubt.
This soul of scoured soil the maker shaped,
Lovingly lengthened his limbs out of the loam,
Brought forth a beautiful body beating with blood;
Breathed on his breath to give birth to a terrible burden
Of perceiving as possible pathways to imperfection.
Adam, alone and alive in absolute freedom,
Listened and learned to love his great liege lord,
Fed on the finest fruits that came to fruition
In forest and field, walking in fear and faith.

Slowly the seasons slipped down the slow stream,
Budding and burgeoning changed to branches bare,
Lithesomely lifting into new living leaf.
Then, for soft shaping of the slumbering soul,
The perpetual presence to Adam perceptibly paled
Into a dream of delight, with dreadful demeanour,
Both loved and, by our first father, fitly feared.

Then, Adam alone called out for almighty aid:
'Bountiful bringer of brightness, I ask you a boon,
Against doubt and despair, against the desolate darkness
That perpetually presses the bounds of my perfect peace.
Needless, I know, a nonsense of mine own kneading,
Pressed into pattern by partial loss of your presence.'
Asked, and was answered; Adam, no longer alone,
Of cloven flesh conceived a companion creature,
Aware as he woke of all her wonderful wildness.

Glendaloch

Strange country this that I am venturing through,
I have not travelled in these realms of thought
Before today, the scents that I have caught
From fragrant bushes, and the flowers, are new.
There is a track that leads under the arch
To a small chapel, where man looks to God
In awe of miracles, be it Moses with his rod,
Or the new green upon the budding larch.

I had thought wonder dead, the city streets
Breathed nothing more of life than life itself,
But in this quiet spot the light completes
Pictures in rock and water; makes the self
Conjoin its inward and its outward spaces
Into one whole, amid these holy places.

Note: Gleann Dá Loch, meaning "glen of two lakes" is a glacial valley in County Wicklow, Ireland. It is renowned for its Early Medieval monastic settlement founded in the 6th century by St Kevin, a hermit priest, and partly destroyed in 1398 by English troops.

Harvest 1938

The insects crowd above the stream,
The sunlight falls across the hill,
Where, under glass, preserved and still,
The ploughman rests behind his team.
The church clock stands nigh on the hour,
Soundless down all the noisy years,
While in the field the heavy ears
Bow, interspersed with poppy flowers.
Young eyes, deep in a wrinkled face,
Evaluate the distant scene,
The turbulent years that lie between
This quiet and that distant place
Reduced to golden hours spun
Of memories kindled by a later sun.

Note: Written in Petworth, West Sussex while looking at a pre-war photograph of a team ploughing and being conscious of an elderly man, who might have been the young ploughman of the photograph, watching me.

Hymn to Pan

Pipe your wild pipes great Pan,
Let revelries
Commence in your deep woods
And greeneries
Entwine about our rustic hostelries.
Pipe your wild pipes great Pan,
Let maidenhood
Be dedicated to the mysteries
Among the trees,
By all our amorous propensities.
Pipe your wild pipes great Pan
And flee
Our hollow towns and all our idle goods,
Between the trees
In some far shady glade to take your ease,
Where, piping still, our weary hearts you please.

Hymn to the Sun

Bountiful beauty of morning, swinging high
Above the illuminated Earth, illustrious globe,
Spreading your light and heat to a lower sphere,
Bringer of blessings and joy, to you we cry.

Fortune and favour we find who darkness fly,
Seeking your light as it shines through the upper air,
Clothed in your rays, as in a mantle or robe,
Seeking transcendent love and burning to die.

Imitation

In the mid-part of mortal journeying,
I, like that other, lost in a dark wood,
Ensnared by faded joys of secondary things,

Determined paths far from the Primal Good,
Though these themselves were innocent and true,
Nothing therein resolved it as it should

And everything was tarnished as it grew.
Blessèd the age when knowledge was confined
In bounds a single mind could clearly view.

Now, truth that's one-year-old is undermined
By its revision; the flux of fixed belief
Makes morals, as with particles, undefined.

Here, while I muse, time, that outrageous thief,
In minutes and in hours steals my days,
And turns my innocence to deadly grief.

The years are wasting in these middle ways,
Becalmed, sea-wracked by underwater weed,
Suns rise and set in the horizon's haze.

Then, in remembrance, crying in my need,
No muse's power invoke, but that great Sun
That made and nurtured both the sapient seed.

I the ascent of the great mount begun,
To sing of Him that encompasses all the worlds,
On Jacob's ladder spring from rung to rung,

Proclaiming the music that the dance unfurls;
Of matter, being and the self that yearns
To purge in fires etern and rise from those wild whorls

Clear seeing, where it dimly now discerns.

Note: See Dante, The Divine Comedy, Canto I of the Inferno.

In Print

The maker of verse, like a mason, with bricks and with mortar lays on
Each elegant course of his structure, in a hundred years it is gone,
Among the good books that lie dog-eared in market or second-hand shop
That the owner is thinking of burning, having never seen anyone stop
To open the musty old pages and breathe in the sweet, stinging air
Which the blood in its morning of singing considered precious and fair
And thought had been captured forever, because the presses turned over
For a privately printed edition embossed with gold on the cover.

Leaving Home

You waved from our joint window as I left
Under the stars that shine perpetually
On faith, or lack of it, habitually
Assumed, or not; and suddenly bereft
In the drift of stars I am lost
And do not know where home is,
Or if my dream of home is the true bliss
I can return to at some finite cost.

Yet, in my doubt, your picture constantly
Rebuffs all unbelief and leads me through
The unquiet hours and unacknowledged cares.
So, beyond logic, all unnaturally
Your image lesser images can undo
And lead me into bliss against my fears.

My Lord is Dead

My Lord is dead.
The mud is deep in English lanes,
The periwinkle in the grass
Is washed by April rains.
Winter secedes to ruthless Spring;
In agony upon the tree,
Its life his death must bring.

Yes, He is dead,
Murdered by me in every sin.
Then how should I assuage the pain,
Then how should I begin.
My Lord is dead.
The church before me stands foursquare,
Confronts me with an open door
And bids me enter there.

My Lord is dead.
The aisle and altar both are bare,
A silent fount of emptiness,
His absence even here.

And then a lightening of the heart,
A certitude the pain imparts.
My Lord is dead,
But, joyously,
The pardon from his open wounds
Is flowing free.

My Lord is dead
And died for me.

Nativity

Brought out of boundless love, bereft of bliss,
From highest heaven, the help of human kind,
Made manifest as man, was born of maid.
The principle of power, made powerless to perform,
His knowledge nullified, he nuzzled the nursing breast.
Still was the night, the silent stars were sown
In crystal clouds across the charcoal clear;
While simple souls sweet adoration showed
And angels amplified his ancient name.

Nocturnal

In early evening hours
When earth and sky and sea
Are dressed in transient brightness
Briefly remember me.

When the storm clouds gather
And all the sky is grey,
I bid you then remember
Our transient bright day.

The short-cropped downland pastures
Trodden by many feet
Cannot for us remember
Where we used to meet.

The moving waters cover
The rocks and then retire;
Our memories are ashes
And ashes our desire.

Lady, all your brightness
Is taken now from me
And all our love is ashes
Strewn on the moving sea.

Northumbrian Poem

There are only the changing seasons
And the wrinkles on a face;
The encouraging sun in the morning
And the evening's glad embrace.
For who can offer us reasons
For the winter sun on a wall,
Wild strawberries eaten in summer
And the curlew's plaintive call.
We dance our lives in slow measure
Of the drift of clouds passed the sun
And take as infinite pleasure
That the dance and the music are one.

Here life is a moment of memory
And a moment of present ease;
The motion of waves on the ocean
And the motion of wind-blown trees.
The clocks and the watches are silent,
The whispering grass has grown tall;
We measure our living and dying
By the winter sun on a wall.
The plinth of the sundial is broken,
The iron encrusted with rust,
A word rests forever unspoken
And lingers between us like dust.

The smoke from the cottages rises
And drifts in the moving air,
While the sudden sea bird surprises
With a call of mournful care.
The church is cool and empty,
With an echoing vast stone floor
And a scent of delicate flowers
That grow on the wind-swept shore.
Here is the delicate pattern,
The growth of death out of birth,
Old bones and dust in a coffer
And a flower out of the earth.

Notting Hill Underground

This the first circle when the whirlwind died,
Cavernous, vast, the rain on an iron lid;
We stand beneath. To permit or forbid
Is nothing here; none of us have cried
To him who bent the arch and tiled the wall.
We are the dead, for we cannot recall
Another place, and no trains run through where
The track's three rails proclaim a thoroughfare.

Nova

Spin gentle globe, before this day is done
Your gentleness, deflowered by the sun,
Shall flame to cinders all across the sky
And charred to ashes all your beauties die.
Consider your hours, were your days well spent
In nurturing grasses, or the transient yew;
Delivering moths, their evening colours blent,
Or making spider webs to deck with dew.

'If for one hour before the light should flare
Into destruction, one could stand and see
Sunlight on water, or in stillness hear
Late autumn leaf fall from deciduous tree,
Then it would justify all I have done,
Though it be broken by the ravenous sun.'

November

The downland wind is thin and shrill,
A lonely tractor ploughs its way,
Turning brown clods beneath the hill;
Autumn, November Saturday.

The onward motion of the Earth
Drives the Sun backward into night
And lights those stars that at His birth
Shone down with undiminished might.

Horse chestnut, ash and beech are bare,
Leaves piled and wet with early rain
Lie underfoot, the sky is clear,
The rushes whisper and complain.

Time turns about November's end
And still turns on to Adventide,
The trees, the spirit, are both blown bare
And in expectancy abide.

The downland wind is thin and chill,
A lonely tractor ploughs its way,
Turning brown clods beneath the hill;
Autumn, November Saturday.

On Lake Mälar

Between two times all things condense into
Sun over water and the harmonies
Of a slight folk song in an unknown tongue.
Yet, if all things remained
Just so, all would be well.

In travelling our origins
Are obscure.
Sun over water and the breaking wave
Give all the meaning that a time can have
Between our active hours.

Words are less than half
The meaning of the water breeze,
For words are doing, when the meaning is
Just out of definition,
Like a half familiar song the hikers sing.

Note: Written on a boat trip from Gripsholm Castle to Stockholm
listening to Swedish students singing folk songs.

Portrait of Persephone

Her fingers lift and turn a page,
Then still and quietly she sits;
Her thought in random motion flits
Backward and forward in its cage.
The room is lighted like a stage
And stubbornly does not admit,
Or even transiently permit,
Another style or other age.
Time ticks upon the mantelpiece
And drops in dust upon the chair,
The drooping ferns are turning brown
And leaf smoke permeates the air;
Her fingers lift to brush her cheek
And brush away a tear.

Rebirth

When the blotched infant from the womb is held
Aloft to encounter life through gummy lids,
The safe secure nest of the amnion he bids
Farewell; as to a world with greater terrors swelled
Than those of birth his sticklike arms extend.
Poor soul, condemned to live a trivial life
In negligible deeds and pointless strife
Before the ignoble and irrelevant end.
Yet at some instant, when he raised his eyes
From pen and book and the ephemeral word,
Time stood suspended in an instant's glory
Of clear cloud shadows on corn and infinite skies,
While, close at hand, in thrilling notes, a bird
Sang out her ancient story.

Recollections of Love

Before the dark is broken and light begins to flow
Across the broken hillside and the grey melting snow,
I'll warm you with my body, 'til soul and body part,
And hymn you with deliberate and ineffectual art.

The cells of both our bodies perish and replace,
For I have lost my virtue, but you have lost your grace.
In recollection's mirror the self you were I see,
But, in your contemplation, do you remember me.

A snowfall out of season has broken all the pines
And a broken prop or rafter has entombed men in the mines,
So a foolish lust or laughter, when the driving joy has paled,
Will delineate disaster and point where we have failed.

Before the dark is broken and light begins to flow
Across the broken hillside and the grey melting snow.
I'll leave you to your weeping, though soul and body part,
And cease, at last, to hymn you with my deliberate art.

Returning

Long after dark, when I am far
From home along the glistening road,
In glancing up I see a star
Racing between the standing clouds.
That star is your's, an onward goad,
Until it stands above the house
Where love with peace makes its abode
And rest endows.

Serenade

Come away softly belovèd, the light is almost gone,
See, they are drawing the curtains, the day is almost done.
Come away softly belovèd, a town is not our place,
Let us arise and depart, to the depths of infinite space.
Come away softly belovèd, lay your head on my breast,
Down the long years belovèd, you in my arms shall rest.
The changing seas will not harm you,
Though the land fall away with the tide,
See how my arms can enfold you
And how at my breast you can hide.
Come away softly belovèd, the night is truly begun,
We are together belovèd, and do not desire the sun.
The day was for yearning and hoping,
Desires too often denied,
But deep in the night my belovèd
We drift on the outgoing tide.

Smoky Mountains

Light in the west, where the sun is sinking,
Glistens on water, dappled with leaves.
The stream and the river, rapidly running
Down to still pools and there lazily lying
Under the shade of the tall forest trees.

Maple and Dogwood, shall I rehearse you,
Name upon name, or shall I tell
Of the sound of water, falling and running,
Of the contours of peaks and the valleys between.

Old Smoky Mountains, how shall I sing you
That song that is woven of light and of water,
Of green and of red and of gold and of blue.
The voice of the river is ever returning
To my inward ear with its call of adieu.

Snow, Frost, Ice

Silent out of a sullen sky they come,
Nursing their intricate nature. Some
On my damp garden slowly melt away,
Where later multitudes will stick and stay.
Forged in symmetric form by that hard frost
Responsible also for a high cost
Of winter residents, who, all summer long,
Sang in the trees their insubstantial song.
Today, the blood lies thick along their veins
In mute despair, the ice has killed the strains
Conceived in frivolous hearts. The burning frost
Envelopes them and their small lives are lost.

Sometimes the Clouds

Sometimes the clouds that gather will not yield
And rain beats both on roof and terrace door,
Thumbs ache and various items are
Mislaid or lost, and that vast emptiness
That lies beneath seems unredeemable.

And yet, all shall be well, because you lie
In everlasting arms and cradled so
See the sun rising over hills so fair
That you could weep for laughing at their green,
In infinite depths of light that linger there.

For love surrounds, even when you cannot see
His present face, or it is deeply hid,
Or marred or spoiled by some intemperate want;
For love endures, triumphant at the end
When sad clouds break to admit the glorious day.

Song

Fierce, fickle folly of love
Display your measure,
Lay out your gaudy toys,
Your tinsel treasure.

Livelong to lie in love,
Or lie alone,
At last all love will lie
Deep under stone.

Fierce, fickle folly of love,
Born out of pleasure,
Shorn of his gaudy toys
Death takes his measure.

The Breaking Ground

Out of the desolate heart of sadness
Starts the unexplainable gladness
Like a bird lifting on light wings
To the dawn heaven where she sings
Her sweetness out across the snow,
Soaring and wheeling, as the joy
Mounts up in us, does not destroy
All that we felt, all that we feared
Age, sickness, death, all that we cared
For broken, lost, or gravely marred,
Ones that we cared for deeply scarred.
No matter, joy mounts up on wings,
In the near hedge the blackbird sings,
While we have smiled in sundry places
And kissed, and crossed the infinite spaces
Between two lonely souls and made
A paradise, where, half afraid
We see the ice melt in the sun,
The rivulets of water run,
The glory spread from field to field,
The new buds burst, the fresh earth yield
Its green of grass, of crops that break
The tilth, of all things come awake,
As glory spreads about us here
At the flushed centre of the year.

The Cheetah

Silent he stands, his ears erect,
Then, with a motion soft and slow,
Glides from his place, smooth through the grass,
Toward the grazing herd below.

No sense of motion in the air,
No thought of danger on the ground,
The cheetah speeds with ears hard back,
The cheetah speeds without a sound.

And desperate in his hurrying haste
The marvellous muscles glide and flow,
The heart beats fast, the breath comes hard,
And silent as a fall of snow.

A sense of panic in the herd,
Antlers buck and hooves beat clay.
He flames through space with deadly glee,
Enveloping his chosen prey.

The Contemplation of Beauty

Let not the stream divide us
With virtuous, purging balm,
And falsify our passion
With its transparent calm.

For tears are joined with laughter,
As thorns and roses are,
And joys are winter sunshine
Seen slanting from afar.

The storm clouds gather and gather,
While Lethe's waters race,
Under a storm of passion
And your remembered face.

The Dead

The night shapes come on steeds of fiery black,
Rearing and snorting, tumbling down my dreams,
The night shapes come, I cannot drive them back
Through Lethe's purging streams.

All of our dead before my eyes are scattered,
These shapes of night, I cannot hold them back,
Asking the cause for which their dying mattered,
Asking the cause or lack.

Dead shapes, night shapes, into my dreams come flying
Bearing ill news, I cannot hold them back;
'While yet you live we are the dying, dying,
Falling from sunlight to the deepest black.'

The night shapes fly on steeds of utter black,
Now from the sunlight each of them is turning.
See how they fly, I cannot hold them back,
No matter how my yearning.

The Deaths of the Poets

Morning and evening, all our intricate days
And intimate evenings, down the narrowing ways
To death's dark portal.

Morning and evening, some I never knew,
But loved, are silent singers under the cold dew
And I am also mortal.

When sleepless night surrounds, the ragged mystery
Is a cold ache from which I would be free
As from a nagging tooth;
Yet, when all's done, as with insensate stones,
The worms will make their detours round my bones.

The Early Sun

Before I woke, the sun before me went
Over the dew-wet grass
And by his new-forged rays a splendour lent
Where the roads pass.

Before I woke, the swallows skimmed the rise
With joyful cries.
They climbed and dipped below the fleecy cloud
In chorus loud.

Before I woke, the day was at its height,
Sunshine and cloud,
Then I arose, went out into the light
And sang aloud.

The Earth has Moved

The earth has moved, the tallest mountains fall,
The deep is troubled, and the waters race
Through a dark cleft to an abysmal place.
Praise then Jehovah, on Jehovah call,
Shout unto God, go clap your hands and tell
His power and wisdom, tell his faithful love;
Great is Jehovah, there is none above,
And nothing I'll fear, because with me he'll dwell.

Come in you people, He is righteousness,
Come in you people, glorify and bless
Your King, who at this sinful world
His kingdom like a mighty rock has hurled
Through man's vain empires, Satan's shadow fame.
Praise God you people, praise his glorious name.

The Earthworks

This Pictish fort, my useful guidebook says,
Was occupied five thousand years ago.
Now, all about the hill, the thick mists blow
Through a pine woodland of these later days.
From this slight summit, if the mist should clear,
The excavated outworks would be seen,
The distant Beauly Firth and, in between,
New, light green, saplings planted out last year.
But now the mists blown back obscure the wood,
Its presence signalled only by the fall
Of myriad drops against the summer leaves.
Enclosed I stand, as that rude watchman stood
In ages past, and listened for the call
Of friend or foe, under the forest eaves.

The Hours of Spring

Nothing save for the sun and sudden sweetness
Of Spring; see the new neatness
Of leaves, lifting, lively and light,
After dawn's dew is dry, all the delight
Of the swift stream, sparkling and springing
Over roots and rocks, rippling and rushing
Between its banks, those all bright bedecked
With flowers of the field, grass finely flecked,
Gold on green, white glistening garlands,
Born in new neatness, of nothing
Save for the sun in sudden sweetness.

The Lack

What would you wish for? A cottage low and white,
Where you can watch the moonglow on the trees
And feed the birds and rabbits on the green?
Deep woods and river, where, in morning light,
Your Bedlingtons can root just as they please,
Sometimes wide ranging, or deep in gorse unseen?

These things you have, and a village too,
A fellowship of believers and of friends,
And useful gifts, to open up and preach
The word of God, as you continue to.
But this one lack remains, a husband who amends
His carelessness, showing reverence at each
Apt moment, so that he can make full clear
That inward love borne for you year-on-year.

The Miraculous Babe

In eternal vigil, waiting still as stone,
Forever in darkness, in sable state alone,
Under unbending branches, bleak and bare,
He guards the stone that guards some treasure there.

Through endless woods, by waters waste and wild,
Down tedious years I sought the miraculous child
And found him not, though often heard him cry
In the midst of marsh, under an icy sky.

Turning aside, time and again I passed
The place where he with features cast
In cold black iron waited evermore
For one to challenge and undo the door.

At last, in age and all with tatters hung,
Beyond endurance, by my failure stung,
I dared the darkness, lifted the bleak gate
To find the glorious babe in shining state.

Note: Written following reading 'The Burning Babe' by Robert
Southwell.

66

The Rainbow

Love refracted in the rainbow,
Love that spans the earth and sky;
God to his creation pledging
His sustaining power and joy.
Now the bow from wrath is resting,
Symbol of God's peace that comes
In the voices of the angels
Praising forth the king of kings.

For the covenant of promise
Is fulfilled in sore distress;
Jesus, Lord, in your compassion
Keep all promises through death.
Thus, as when the sacred rainbow
Is reborn from storm and rain,
So through your despair and sorrow
Are we raised without a stain.

Not us only, all creation
Lifted high on eagles' wings
Rises up to meet in glory
You the lord of everything.
Nevermore to be forsaken,
Never more be left alone,
But in joy to praise for ever
Him who reigns upon the throne.

Note: Written as a hymn to be sung at a service at which my wife
preached on the covenant between God and Noah.

The Rider

The trees are heavy with apples,
The straw is dry in the barn,
The leaves sweep over the autumn
And drift by a wall on the farm.
The trees are bare by the Ridgeway,
The hill fort is bleak on the down,
The moon is but recently risen
And lights are on in the town.
The rider upon his black stallion
Has ridden this pathway before,
Has stopped at the lonely cottage,
Or knocked at the farmhouse door.
The hooves of his great horse are silent,
Though he gallops remorselessly on;
No one knows when the rider approaches,
Or lets out his breath when he's gone.
The trees are heavy with apples,
The straw is dry in the barn,
A light shining bright in a window
Is full of comfort and calm;
But the rider gallops unceasing
And passes the farm on the hill,
For no man measures his going
And even the dogs lie still.

The Seasons

First, misty morns, in mildness, swiftly bring
Attendant flowers, birds that in chorus sing
Melodiously, to welcome fruitful spring.

Now, joyfully, the early rising sun
Jousts with the clouds that ever swiftly run
Across the sky, as summer is begun.

Slowly the declining, shortening days
Of autumn stain with leaves the country ways
Nor cease until trees their stark branches raise.

Dark, damp and drear at last the seasons send
Jaundiced and jaded at the old year's end
Foul fog and frost, as winter's short days wend.

The Squall

We own no haven love, nor are we blest
With quiet seas. Tossed by each monstrous swell,
We snatch at fragile stillnesses that dwell
Between the waves by which we are oppressed.
But, though we meet with dangers yet unguessed
And are estranged by circumstance or chance,
In all our pain love's boundaries advance,
As our new timbers to their task are stressed.

I watch you sleeping, never shall I be
Far from your side, for all I range abroad.
The gale is all blown out, a gentle swell
Throws gleams of sunshine from the peaceful sea,
Our craft, sea anchored, rock in slow accord,
And hulls, so nearly sundered, are made well.

The Still Centre

Are the scents softer and the stars more bright,
And the late animals more noiseless still
Than they were that last time, in the twilight,
I stood upon this hill.

Scents are not softer, stars are not more bright,
But the memory is longer, can recall
More turbulence, more moments of delight
Of winter and fall.

The scents of twilight dominate the will,
Opposed to circumstance they bring delight,
With passion over-ridden the heart is still
And welcomes night.

The Summer Storm

The wind is full of rain
And it is dark.
My soul, where is our ark
To float above the pain;
The night is dark,
The wind is full of rain.

My soul, we bear a stain;
In this we both are one
And share the pain.

To envelope us an evil web was spun,
We span, did not refrain
And it was done,
And is the pain.
No use to wish that we had not begun,
Or to complain
That now our night is dark
And full of rain.

Lord help us taken the strain
To break this net,
Thrice multiply the pain
And thus beget
Us whole and one again.
For now our night is dark,
The wind is full of rain.

Now there is silence, except in the heart,
But that, recalcitrant, must rant and rave,
And ever claim an influential part,
Until its pulse is buried in the grave.

Would that my heart were still
And was not moved
By sundry passions,
Driven only by Thy will.
Would that my heart were still.

My staggering footsteps to deceit are strayed
And tottering, stumbling, perish in the grave;
There, in the dark, I scream 'I am afraid',
Which no-one hears.
Shall these, my fears,
Be buried in that grave?

Merlin lies sleeping in a hidden cave,
Atlantis sleeps beneath the gliding wave,
And all things come to rest
At Thy behest,
And still I am afraid.

For all my sins will catch me out at last
And what I thought was past will not be past.
I, in that second grave, will surely lie,
A second and a final death to die.

I fear, that God exists and knows my soul,
That God is not, which leaves the black abyss
Of being other people's memories
And playing the example as a role.

Here there is silence, except in the heart,
And that, recalcitrant, must rant and rave,
Fearing its death in its two sundry graves.
Here there is silence
Except in the heart.

I hear the water and the wind in trees,
And the high stars are bright above the sky.
This the true silence, now the heart is still,
My soul belongs to God, my body to my will.
In death, we shed our sin with the disease,
For both have played their part when bodies die;
Then all things come to rest
At Your behest,
For in your consolation, comforted they lie.

The Turning Tide

Rheged and Elmet; two great armies;
Sun on shield with the flash of bronze.
Rheged and Elmet, two great armies,
Waiting in arms.

Over the fields the horsemen are riding,
Sun on spear with a silver gleam.
Over the fields the horsemen are riding,
Over the stream.

Urien of Rheged, battle leader,
High his banner, the dragon red,
Streams in the breeze of a springtime morning,
Overhead.

Far in the lengthening views of sunrise
A mighty dark roles over the ground;
Muted, grumbling, thunder approaching;
Barbarian sound.

'Come my brave hunters, polish your spear points,
Repin the leather upon your shields,
Tonight we will sing in the halls of our fathers,
Or lie in the fields.'

'See how our leaders go forth in the vanguard;
Each cloak of crimson, each circlet of gold.
Slingman and axman, swordsman and spearman,
Be bold.'

'See the wild Saxon, bare-bosomed and smiling,
High in the air he wields his great sword.
Around him our kinsmen have fallen, are dying,
Bloodily gored.'

In one revolution, the red earth spurning,
A youth of courage (none knows his name)
Dives through the melee and guts the wild foeman
With blade of flame.

Now it is evening, the daylight is fading,
The sun is lying, red, in the west.
Rheged and Elmet, armies victorious,
Rest.

For me, I am dying, alone on a hillside,
The wound in my side throbs dully with pain
And I will return to my home and my kinfolk
Never again.

There in the hall they are singing of triumph,
Sun on shield and brave banner of red.
Tomorrow they'll come, with priests and shovels,
To bury their dead.

Together

Quietly they together lie
Her hand in his.
Under Orion who wheels in the sky
And the wind-bent trees.
There in quiet darkness they lie,
Her hand in his.

The roar of the sea on the shore
And the cry of a bat
Are lost in a blanket of stone
And nothing amiss
Can trouble the touch of bone on bone,
Her hand in his.

Two O'Clock

These are the quiet hours, when the night begins to wane
And my soul beats against the flesh as wind against the pane,
The hours when other, quieter, souls slumber on like death
And I measure the beating of the clock against each in-drawn breath.

The streets are empty, each passing whore
Has gathered her quarry and gone,
While I am left here to tot up the score
And consolation have none.

These are the quiet hours, when the night begins to wane,
While the window murmurs my sorrows against the window pane.

Van Gogh

Warm russet cloth, warm look, warm youthful flesh,
The westering sun upon a red-flagged floor,
White-painted chairs, a table, a green cloth
And wine in a dark bottle, nothing more.

October is your month, late summer's breath,
A scatter of leaves blown down, a taste of death,
To set against your ripe fecundity.

To see, to touch, to clasp, feel the warm mouth,
This wine full blooded with the summer sun,
This clean-limbed parlour, lit by a shaft of light,
And all the voluptuous beauty of the south.

Walking Tour

The quiet villages that lie
Slumberous between the fields of wheat,
Beneath an infinite depth of sky,
Are sweet.

Sweet to the traveller's weary limbs,
That have climbed over the billowy down;
In shimmering air the swallow skims
The crown.

Crown of long toil on crowded ways,
Of office hours and busy streets,
In recompense, these few snatched days
Of country treats.

Treats of the peace of woods and fields,
Slow-moving sun and sudden showers,
The granary that harvest yields
And summer flowers.

Waterloo Line

Now stands the sun high hot above the hill
And morning mists repair to darkling streams.
From plain to downland, trains with temperate will
Head on to Dorking, Leatherhead and Cheam.
Once more, in darkness, rolling rumbling wheels
Carry us further from the jostling wen,
Passed Box Hill, with its upthrust chalky keel,
From downland to the Sussex plain again.
Sometimes, a doe, driven startled through the woods,
Or rabbit, ears up-pricked in field of grain,
Or gulls uprising from the furrowed soil,
Signal the recognition of our train.
Sometimes, black darkness, split by station lights,
While gusts of rain splatter the greasy panes,
We sit in smoky silence with our books,
Enduring the oppression of the train.

William Blake

He walked naked in his garden
But the evening had grown cold,
While the mind that dreamed of Albion
Was weary, lone and old.

For heaven and hell were empty,
And no angel came over the sea,
As Blake stooped in his garden
Under the gnarled oak tree.

Yet once more came the thunder
Roaring out of the west
And Satan stood in his garden
Baring his flaming breast,
While the stars fell down in showers
And the trees were tipped with flame
As all the hosts of heaven
Praised his eternal name.